LIFE CYCLES

Sunflower

Ruth Thomson

WAYLAND

Explore the world with **Popcorn** - your complete first non-fiction library.

Look out for more titles in the **Popcorn** range. All books have the same format of simple text and awesome images. Text is carefully matched to the pictures to help readers to identify and understand key vocabulary.
www.waylandbooks.co.uk/popcorn

First published in 2009 by Wayland

Copyright © Wayland 2009

Wayland
Hachette Children's Books
338 Euston Road
London NW1 3BH

Wayland Australia
Level 17/207 Kent Street
Sydney NSW 2000

Managing Editor: Victoria Brooker
Concept designer: Paul Cherrill

British Library Cataloguing in Publication Data:
Thomson, Ruth
 Sunflower. - (Popcorn: Life Cycles)
 1. Sunflower - Life cycles - Juvenile literatur
 I Title
571.8'2399

ISBN: 978 07502 5783 1

Printed and bound in China

Wayland is a division of Hachette Children's Books,
an Hachette Livre UK Company.

www.hachettelivre.co.uk

Photographs:
Cover, title page, 4, 5 Aflo/naturepl.com;
2, 13, 16 Nature Production/naturepl.com;
6 © James McQuillan/istockphoto.com;
6 (inset) Adam White/naturepl; 7 ©
Bobhdeering/Alamy; 8 © Nigel
Cattlin/Alamy; 9 © Nigel Cattlin/Alamy;
10 © Elena Elisseeva/istockphoto.com;
11, 12, 17 Papilio; 14 © Matej
Michelizza/istockphoto.com; 15
osf/photolibrary.com; 18 David
Shale/naturepl; 19 © zoran
simin/istockphoto.com; 20
Bildarchiv/Photolibrary.com; 21© Ron
Watts/CORBIS

Contents

What are sunflowers?

Sunflowers are tall flowering plants.
In summer, their large flowers have lots
of bright yellow petals.

A sunflower
can grow as
tall as your
classroom.

Sunflowers always turn towards
the sun and follow it wherever
it is in the sky.

Planting seeds

Every sunflower starts as a seed.
The seed coat is hard and dry.
This protects the seed inside.

seed

seed coat

Sunflower seeds are good to eat.
Birds find the seeds tasty, too.

Sunflower seeds
can be used to
make cooking oil
and margarine.

Roots grow

In spring, people plant the seeds in warm, damp soil. The hard seed coat splits. A root appears.

The root grows down into the soil.

Smaller roots sprout from the main root. The roots have tiny hairs. These take in water from the soil.

A sunflower seed needs water, air and warmth to grow.

9

A shoot sprouts

A shoot grows upwards. It breaks
through the soil into the open air.

seed coat

Two seed leaves open out.
These are small and plump.

These seed leaves contain food for the growing shoot.

Leaves appear

The shoot grows taller. New leaves appear. These leaves use sunlight, water and air to make food.

Can you see how the leaves grow in pairs?

stem

The plant grows taller. The stem
is thick and strong. More leaves sprout.
The roots grow longer and spread
out to hold the plant firmly
in the ground.

Flowers open

A flower bud grows at the top of the stem.

Green sepals protect the petals inside.

Slowly, the sepals unfold.

petals

sepal

leaf

stem

What can you see under the sepals?

The sunflower opens. Its flower-head
is made up of hundreds of tiny flowers.
These are called florets.

Bees pollinate

The bright yellow petals attract bees.
They come to feed on nectar. As they crawl
over the florets, they become covered with pollen.

When the bees fly to other sunflowers, they brush some of the pollen onto other florets. This is called pollination.

Can you see how bees carry pollen?

Bees take pollen back to their nest as food.

Seeds grow

Once the florets are pollinated, the petals wilt and fall off. The leaves shrivel and turn brown. Tiny seeds begin to swell.

Soon the flower head is full of seeds.
The ripe seeds make the
flower head so heavy that
it droops over.

Each flower head
can have as many
as 1,000 seeds.

From seed to sunflower

As the flower-head dries some seeds fall out.
Birds come to feed on the seeds,
but they often drop some.

These seeds may grow into
new sunflowers next spring.

Sunflower life cycle

In spring, a seed is planted. First it grows a root, then a shoot. Soon leaves and a flower appear. After pollination, seeds begin to grow.

seeds
A seed is planted.

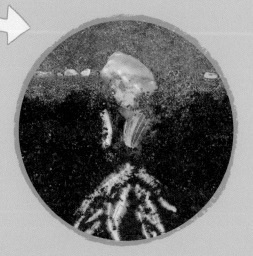

roots and shoot
Roots grow down in the ground then a shoot grows up.

flowers
The petals fall off and seeds grow.

flowers and leaves
Leaves grow and a flower bud and petals appear.

Make a paper plate sunflower

You will need:
- paper plate
- yellow crêpe paper
- green card
- scissors
- glue

Make a colourful sunflower to brighten up a room.

1. Cut out lots of big petals from yellow crêpe paper.

2. Cover a paper plate with glue. Stick down a ring of petals.

3. Overlap another ring of petals on top. Crumple the leftover scraps into balls. Glue them into a circle of florets in the centre of the plate.

4. Roll green crêpe paper into a stem. Tape it to the back of the plate.

5. You could make several sunflowers to give to your friends.

Glossary

bud the top of a shoot that will open and grow into a leaf or flower

floret a tiny flower in a flower head

flower head a flower made up of lots of tiny florets

nectar the sweet liquid inside a flower that attract insects

pollen the yellow grains of powder inside a flower

root the part of a plant that grows down into the ground and takes in water

sepals the green flaps that protect a flower bud

shrivel to dry up and die

stem the stalk of a plant. Leaves and flowers grow on the stem.

Index